Understanding
Mission

Understanding Mission

A Study Guide for the Church

Christopher J. H. Wright

brought to you by

Langham
PARTNERSHIP

© 2025 Christopher J. H. Wright

Published 2025 by Langham Global Library
An imprint of Langham Publishing
www.langhampublishing.org

Langham Publishing and its imprints are a ministry of Langham Partnership

Langham Partnership
PO Box 296, Carlisle, Cumbria, CA3 9WZ, UK
www.langham.org

ISBNs:
978-1-78641-201-0 Print

British Library Cataloguing-in-Publication Data
A catalogue record for this book is available from the British Library

ISBN: 978-1-78641-201-0

Cover & Book Design: projectluz.com

Contents

For

Jenny Brown

Who, as World Mission Minister at All Souls, Langham Place
invited me to preach on the Five Marks of Mission
in September 2010,
a sermon which generated
several lectures, a book, and this Study Course

Introduction

Welcome to this course of studies on "Understanding Mission." These studies can be worked on individually, but "for best results" (as they say), it will be far more profitable to use them in small groups who have committed themselves to working together through the course over a period of weeks or months. Learning together is a great way to encourage one another in personal growth, maturity, and our calling – both as individuals and as churches – to be "on mission" for God

The word "mission" is a very flexible term! For some, it refers only to overseas missionaries and agencies; for others, "missions" are local evangelistic outreach programmes or events. Many Christians see mission as something that other people are called and sent out to do, and they are happy to support such fine people in their work through giving and prayer. This course, however, is built on the conviction that mission is the calling, responsibility, privilege, and joy of the whole church and all its members in all their lives as disciples of Jesus Christ and that all our mission as God's people flows from, and participates in, the mission of God himself.

However, it is not easy to shift from the perspective of "mission as something other people do" to "mission is what the whole church – including me – exists for!" This shift can only happen through careful attention to the whole Bible – not just the few "missionary verses" that feature on World Mission Sunday or in brochures and posters related to a church's overseas mission activities.

Getting our heads around the whole Bible for "Understanding Mission" is a big challenge. It requires intentional effort and commitment to think things through together with others, especially if God has called us to any form of leadership among his people. We must not only ask, "What does the Bible as a whole say about God's mission – that is, God's plan and purpose for his whole world?" but also, "What are the implications for us as God's people in the world today? Who are we (the church), and what are we here for?" These are big questions! And that's because God has a big mission, and we have a big gospel. But if you're willing to have a go at answering such questions, this course will not only stretch your thinking but also, we hope, motivate and encourage you to re-evaluate how you and your church *think* about mission. It will also help you to consider some *practical* steps you can take, both as individuals and as a church, in light of what you work on together in this course.

Although this course is structured around eight sessions, each with an accompanying video, participants may find that some sessions contain more content than can be adequately discussed and acted upon in a single session. Please try to remain flexible and be willing to spread the load. For instance, if the discussion during a particular session is going well but you have not covered all the material, consider saying, "Let's come back to this topic again at our next meeting to tackle the remaining texts and questions." It's better to take your time and dig deep than to skim over these important biblical themes too shallowly. Adopting a flexible approach is more likely to lead to greater satisfaction within the group and produce more lasting outcomes in practice.

The content of this course has been developed on the basis of my recently published book, *The Great Story and the Great Commission: Participating in the Biblical Drama of Mission* (Baker, 2023). This course is not a study guide to that book as such, but it reflects the same purpose and flow. Ideally, the course and the book work together as companions, but equally, each can be used and read on their own. At the end of each session in the course, there is a section that encourages participants to dig deeper by reading a relevant portion of *The Great Story and the Great Commission*. And at the end of the whole course you will find more resources for those who want to think and explore even further in the field of Christian mission theology. *Group leaders* especially are strongly encouraged, if they can, to get hold of a copy of *The Great Story and the Great Commission* and to read the recommended pages for each session, and to watch the relevant video before each session, in order to be well prepared to steer the discussion most profitably.

There are also several quotations from *The Cape Town Commitment*, which is the statement from the Third Lausanne Congress on World Evangelization, Cape Town, 2010. You can get a copy of this as a standalone booklet edition or the Study Edition edited by Rose Dowsett, which includes additional material and discussion questions. Both these resources are available from any reputable bookseller. Alternatively, you can read this for free online or download it as a PDF from the Lausanne website: https://lausanne.org/statement/ctcommitment.

The Sessions

Each study session includes three main components, following some very brief (just two or three minutes) starter questions:

1. Watch a short video talk by Chris Wright, introducing and surveying the theme of the session.

2. Read Bible passages that are relevant to that theme and engage in group discussion around a number of questions that follow (this will take up the bulk of the time).

3. Pray together for God's help in building what has been learned into our lives, both individually and in the life of our church.

Notes to Group Leaders

- This is a *Study* Guide! So please encourage your participants to do some reading and study on their own beforehand (maybe even insist on this!). Ideally, group members should come to each session having read the Bible passages given in the session notes, and having done some initial thinking about the questions. Such diligent preparation and homework by all the participants will lead to much more fruitful discussions than just a "cold start" each time. It will enable the best use of the discussion time. It will also foster mutual commitment within the group and encourage everyone to think, "This is a challenge that we're all working on together, so I'll come to each session well-prepared."

- As Group Leader, of course, you want to lead by example! So we recommend that you try to obtain a copy of *The Great Story and the Great Commission* for yourself. As I said, it provides the broader biblical foundations on which this course is built. You will find it most helpful, in preparing for each session, to read the recommended pages of that book that are noted at the end of each session. Similarly, if you watch the video yourself before playing it in the group session, it will help you be better prepared for how people respond in the discussion that follows.

- Most sessions include a "warm-up" question intended for use at the beginning of the session to get people talking. The aim of this question is to bring to the surface some of what people already think. So, don't allow this initial discussion go on for more than a few minutes before getting into the meat of the study.

- The notes for each session provide a range of questions around key discussion areas. Please don't feel that you have to ask every single question in strict order or wait for answers to each one! These questions are there to guide and shape the conversation. You may choose to focus on some questions more than others and you may craft your own follow-up questions. You may ask the group to reflect on some questions on their own.

- As suggested earlier, be prepared to spread some topics over two sessions rather than rushing through and leaving people frustrated by a lack of depth. We fully recognize that there is a lot of content in this course and some will find it demanding. All the more reason to let the discussions dig deeply and take the time it needs.

- Do keep an eye on the time. People need to know that they won't be there all night! Try to leave enough time to tackle any important application questions that may come up towards the end of each study.

- It's important to involve different group members in reading the Bible passages. However, be considerate, and remember that some people may be uncomfortable reading aloud (for example, dyslexia may be a challenge for some or English may not be a first language for others). Don't pressure people, but ask if they would be comfortable reading a passage – and try to do so before the session begins. And of course, if people are encouraged to read the passages beforehand, there will be less need to read them aloud during the session. But people do need to have their Bibles open.

- Please remember to allow time for prayer at the end of each session. It's important not to just "blow the whistle" on the discussion and have everyone break up and go home (or grab the refreshments!). People need to spend a few minutes in quiet reflection, letting the Holy Spirit work, allowing the impact of the time spent discussing God's word sink in, turning their thoughts into prayer, and then moving from prayer into action.

Digging Deeper

There's only so much one can cover in a short course like this, with input from the video talks and group study of the Bible. Much more has been written on the theme of Christian mission, including some of my other books. The two titles that most strongly reinforce the convictions of this course are my *The Mission of God: Unlocking the Bible's Grand Narrative* (IVP, 2nd edition, October 2025) and *The Mission of God's People: A Biblical Theology of the Church's Mission* (Zondervan, 2010).

For group leaders, group members, or church leaders interested in following up on this course through further and wider reading, a list of additional resources is provided at the end of Session 8.

Session 1

Whose Mission? Whose Story?

In this first study we will think about shifting our thinking about mission from something we do (primarily), to recognizing that the Bible shows us God *himself* on mission, with a goal and purpose to achieve - in which he calls us to participate.

Brief Starter Questions

What does the word "mission" immediately bring to mind, and what lies behind these associations?

_____

_____

_____

What Bible verses do you associate with mission, and why those verses in particular?

_____

_____

_____

Video

Watch the video for Session 1.

Discussion

> Our proper starting point in thinking about mission *biblically* should be first of all *the mission of God,* the divine sovereign purpose that is the prime governing theme of the whole Bible narrative. What does the Bible tell us about the overarching plan and purpose of God for the whole creation and the human race? Only when we have got hold of that should we go on to ask (as we must) the follow-up question, "What then is the mission of God's people, as we participate in the mission of God himself?" Who are we and what are we here for?
>
> *The Great Story and the Great Commission,* page 65

† 1. Read Ephesians 1:9–10

According to Paul, what is the ultimate will or plan or purpose of God? Does the achievement of that goal depend on us or on God? What does this say about the nature and scope of our mission?

_____

_____

_____

† 2. Read Romans 8:18–25

What is the "end of the story" both for creation and for us? What, then, is "the hope" that we have, and how does this connect with the longing of creation?

_____

_____

_____

[≡?] Where does "mission" fit into the scenario that Paul paints here?

_____

_____

_____

_____

[†] 3. Read Revelation 21:1–5 and 22:1–5

Revelation 21–22 are "the *end* of the story" of the Bible (though, of course, they are really a new beginning in God's renewed creation).

[≡?] In these verses, what echoes do you see of "the *beginning* of the story" in Genesis?

_____

_____

_____

_____

[≡?] What does this tell us about God's intention (his mission) for our ongoing life in the new creation as pictured in Revelation?

_____

_____

_____

4. Read this extract from The Cape Town Commitment

Although I refer to this extract from *The Cape Town Commitment* in the video, it would be helpful to read it aloud together as you come to the end of your session. Notice how quickly it moves from *our* language of "world mission" to outlining what the Bible says is "the mission *of God*" – all the sentences that describe with what *God* plans to do.

We are committed to world mission, because it is central to our understanding of God, the Bible, the Church, human history and the ultimate future. The whole Bible reveals the mission of God to bring all things in heaven and earth into unity under Christ, reconciling them through the blood of his cross. In fulfilling his mission, God will transform the creation broken by sin and evil into the new creation in which there is no more sin or curse. God will fulfil his promise to Abraham to bless all nations on the earth, through the gospel of Jesus, the Messiah, the seed of Abraham. God will transform the fractured world of nations that are scattered under the judgment of God into the new humanity that will be redeemed by the blood of Christ from every tribe, nation, tongue and language, and will be gathered to worship our God and Saviour. God will destroy the reign of death, corruption and violence when Christ returns to establish his eternal reign of life, justice and peace. Then God, Immanuel, will dwell with us, and the kingdom of the world will become the kingdom of our Lord and of his Christ and he shall reign for ever and ever.

The Cape Town Commitment, I.10

As you read this extract, how many echoes of Scripture – from both the Old and New Testaments – can you hear? Each time someone offers an answer to this question, pause to reflect on how it might affect what we think *our* mission should be.

5. Pulling it together

We will have a lot more to think about as we bring the whole Bible story to bear on the way we understand mission. For now, however, consider the following questions:

How has this first study affected or changed the way you would answer the questions in the brief starter questions at the beginning?

_____

_____

_____

_____

If you were drawn into a conversation about "mission" at your church, what might you now want to say?

_____

_____

_____

_____

Digging Deeper

The Great Story and the Great Commission
Read: chapter 4, pages 64–67 and chapter 1, pages 1–11

Session 2

The Missional Drama of Scripture – Part 1

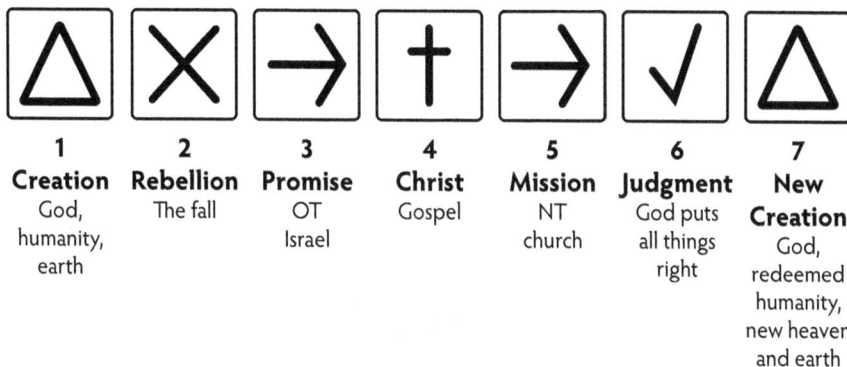

△	✕	→	†	→	✓	△

1	2	3	4	5	6	7
Creation	**Rebellion**	**Promise**	**Christ**	**Mission**	**Judgment**	**New**
God,	The fall	OT	Gospel	NT	God puts	**Creation**
humanity,		Israel		church	all things	God,
earth					right	redeemed
						humanity,
						new heaven
						and earth

The above figure that depicts "The Seven Acts of the Biblical Drama" is inspired by the work of Craig Bartholomew and Michael Goheen, in their book, *The Drama of Scripture*, who built upon the analogy first presented by N. T. Wright, presenting the Bible as a great drama in 6 acts.

In this session, we will be thinking about the first three "acts" of the great drama of Scripture, all of which come in the Old Testament: Creation (questions 1 and 2), Rebellion (question 3), and God's promise of blessing for all nations through his chosen people, Israel (questions 4 and 5). Try to pace your discussion to allow adequate time for the last two questions.

Brief Starter Questions

Have you ever heard, or when did you last hear, a sermon about mission based on an Old Testament text?

_____

_____

_____

Why does it sometimes seem as if the Old Testament is irrelevant for Christian mission?

_____

_____

_____

Video

Watch the video for Session 2.

Discussion

1. Creation: Read Genesis 1:26–28 and 2:15, and Revelation 5:10 and 22:3–4

> It is important to take this first act of the Bible story very seriously, as the foundation for all the rest. If we don't have a strong grasp of the creational *beginning* of the story and all it means for human life, societies and cultures, we will not have a good understanding of the *goal* of the rest of the story, and its wonderful *ending* in the new creation. Indeed, one reason for the weakness and narrowness of much that passes

for "mission" in some churches and among some evangelical Christians, is a woefully inadequate theology of creation.

The Great Story and the Great Commission, page 18

What does the balance of "rule" and "serve" in the responsibility given by God to human beings in Genesis 1 and 2 teach us about our mission on earth? In other words, what is God's mission for us as human beings, not just as Christians (since we don't stop being human beings when we become Christians)?

_____

_____

_____

_____

Revelation says that we will continue to "reign" and "serve" like kings and priests on the earth in God's new creation (Rev 5:10; 22:3–5). If this is what lies ahead for us in the new creation (we'll be busy!), how do you think this prospect could influence the way we live and work in this creation, where God has already placed us to "rule" and "serve"?

_____

_____

_____

_____

2. Creation: Read this extract from The Cape Town Commitment

The Bible shows us God's truth about human work as part of God's good purpose in creation. The Bible brings the whole of our working lives within the sphere of ministry, as we serve God in different callings. By contrast, the falsehood of a "sacred-secular divide" has permeated the Church's thinking and action. This divide tells us that religious activity belongs to God, whereas other activity does not. Most Christians spend most of their time in work which they may think has little spiritual value (so-called secular work). But God is Lord of *all* of life. "Whatever you do, work at it with all your heart, as working for the Lord, not for men," said Paul, to slaves in the pagan workplace (Col 3:23).

In spite of the enormous evangelistic and transformational opportunity of the workplace, where adult Christians have most relationships with non-Christians, few churches have the vision to equip their people to seize this. We have failed to regard work in itself as biblically and intrinsically significant, and we have failed to bring the whole of life under the Lordship of Christ.

We name this secular-sacred divide as a major obstacle to the mobilization of all God's people in the mission of God, and we call upon Christians worldwide to reject its unbiblical assumptions and resist its damaging effects. We challenge the tendency to see ministry and mission (local and cross-cultural) as being mainly the work of church-paid ministers and missionaries, who are a tiny percentage of the whole body of Christ.

We encourage all church members to accept and affirm their own daily ministry and mission as being wherever God has called them to work. We challenge pastors and church leaders to support people in such ministry – in the community and in the workplace – "to equip the saints for works of service [ministry]" – in every part of their lives.

We need intensive efforts to train all God's people in whole-life discipleship, which means to live, think, work, and speak from a biblical worldview and with missional effectiveness in every place or circumstance of daily life and work.

The Cape Town Commitment, IIA.3

To what extent do you agree with those points?

_____

_____

_____

_____

What difference should it make if all Christians learned to see their daily work (not just paid employment, but whatever work they engage in from day to day) as God's calling and part of their mission as they live within God's created order?

_____

_____

_____

_____

Here's how John Stott puts it:

> It is a wonderful privilege to be a missionary or a pastor, *if God calls us to it.* But it is equally wonderful to be a Christian lawyer, industrialist, politician, manager, social worker, television script-writer, journalist, or home-maker, *if God calls us to it.* . . . There is a crying need for Christian men and women who see their daily work as their primary Christian ministry and who determine to penetrate their secular environment for Christ.
>
> John Stott, *The Contemporary Christian* (IVP, 1991), pages 140–142; italics original

Is that how members of the group "see their daily work" – as their ministry and the mission to which God has called them? We will return to this point in the final session, so don't spend too much time on it now – keep moving along.

✝ 3. Rebellion: Read Genesis 6:5, 11–13

In light of Genesis 6:5, 11–13, read these two extracts from *The Cape Town Commitment* and *The Great Story and the Great Commission*.

We love the good news in a world of bad news. The gospel addresses the dire effects of human sin, failure and need. Human beings rebelled against God, rejected God's authority and disobeyed God's Word. In this sinful state, we are alienated from God, from one another and from the created order. Sin deserves God's condemnation. Those who refuse to repent and 'do not obey the gospel of our Lord Jesus Christ will be punished with eternal destruction and shut out from the presence of God' (2 Thess 1:9). The effects of sin and the power of evil have corrupted every dimension of human personhood (spiritual, physical, intellectual and relational). They have permeated cultural, economic, social, political and religious life through all cultures and all generations of history. They have caused incalculable misery to the human race and damage to God's creation. Against this bleak background, the biblical gospel is indeed very good news.

The Cape Town Commitment, I.8.a

> Genesis 4–11 goes on to show how sin impacts not just individual and relational life, but also grows and escalates through the generations and centuries of history, spreads to societies and nations, leads to corruption and violence, infects all cultures, creates division and confusion among nations, and has also brought damage and frustration to creation. Sin has pervaded the structures of human society, hardened and entrenched as they are through historical longevity and cultural approval.
>
> *The Great Story and the Great Commission,* page 21

Against the background of this radical and comprehensive analysis of the reality of sin and evil, why is it *important* to take seriously the personal nature of sin (that is, that we are all *individually* sinners) but also recognize that this is *insufficient* in itself for our concept and practice of mission? In other words, we know it is important that the Bible says every one of us is individually a sinner; but why is that not enough?

_____

_____

_____

_____

What else does the Bible say about sin and evil in human life and the created order?

_____

_____

_____

_____

What difference should the awareness of that wider understanding of sin make to our mission? What should our mission involve in full awareness and response to all that?

_____

_____

_____

_____

4. God's Promise: Read the following texts, one after the other

It would be good to invite group members who are comfortable doing so to read the following passages out loud one after the other. This is just a small selection of Bible texts that speak about God's plan for all nations – that is, the mission of God, in fulfilment of his promise to Abraham.

Psalm 22:27

Psalm 86:8–10

Zechariah 2:10–11

Galatians 3:7–9*;

Romans 15:8–12*;

Revelation 7:9–10

* In these two passages, where the English translation says "Gentiles," read "the nations" (for that is what the word means, as in the Great Commission).

Why do so many Christians who claim to be "biblical" neglect the Bible's emphasis on "all nations"?

_____

_____

_____

_____

How does this great vision of God's plan for all nations encourage us as we play our part in the global mission of the church?

_____

_____

_____

_____

5. God's Promise: Mission in the light of the Old Testament

What difference will it make to how you and your church think about and engage in mission if you begin to pay more attention to the *promises* of God and the *people* of God in the *Old Testament* as well as the New Testament? Might you even consider preaching a mission sermon from the Old Testament now?!

_____

_____

_____

_____

The following extracts may help you as think about how to answer that question.

[The Old Testament] is a huge library of books! But remember – it is all "moving forward," like a great journey, based on God's promise, and highlighting God's redemption, grace and faithfulness, and always pointing towards a future destination. ... And through all its narratives, laws, songs and prophecies, the Old Testament is a single story that is all moving in one direction towards its destiny in Christ.

So then, God's promise and Israel's hope drive the Bible story forward through the history of Israel in the Old Testament era – Act 3. Israel constantly fails to live up to their covenant commitment to their God. But even through multiple episodes of judgement followed by grace and restoration, God keeps the story "on course" towards the fulfilment of his promise.

The Great Story and the Great Commission, page 26

God calls his people to share his mission. The Church from all nations stands in continuity through the Messiah Jesus with God's people in the Old Testament. With them we have been called through Abraham and commissioned to be a blessing and a light to the nations. With them, we are to be shaped and taught through the law and the prophets to be a community of holiness, compassion and justice in a world of sin and suffering. We have been redeemed through the cross and resurrection of Jesus Christ, and empowered by the Holy Spirit to bear witness to what God has done in Christ. The Church exists to worship and glorify God for all eternity and to participate in the transforming mission of God within history. Our mission is wholly derived from God's mission, addresses the whole of God's creation, and is grounded at its centre in the redeeming victory of the cross. This is the people to whom we belong, whose faith we confess and whose mission we share.

The Cape Town Commitment, I.10.a

Digging Deeper

The Great Story and the Great Commission
Read: Chapter 2, pages 12–27

Session 3

The Missional Drama of Scripture – Part 2

In this session, we will be thinking about the other four "acts" of the great drama of Scripture – the ones that unfold in the New Testament. One act is past history (Act 4: Christ in the Gospels); one has been ongoing in the past and present, and will continue until Christ returns (Act 5: The mission of the church since Pentecost); and two are still future (Act 6: The final judgement, and Act 7: The new creation).

Brief Starter Question

Jesus said, "As you [Father] sent me into the world, so I am sending them into the world" (John 17:18, repeated at 20:21). In the light of that, what would make *Christmas* a good time to preach about mission?

_____

_____

_____

Video

Watch the video for Session 3.

As you watched the video, I hope you caught the point that *all* of these "acts" in the drama of Scripture are relevant to our mission because they are all part of God's mission – accomplished in Christ, ongoing through history, and to be completed in the new creation. In this session, we need to flesh that out a bit and think about how this whole story should shape our understanding and practice of mission.

Discussion
† 1. Read John 20:19–23

Jesus makes a clear connection between how *he* was sent by the Father "into the world" and how he sends *us* "into the world." That means that we need to pay close attention to everything the Gospels tell us about how *Jesus* accomplished *his* mission when we are trying to grasp what *our* mission should involve. Act 4 (Christ in the Gospels) is central to the whole drama of Scripture and must, therefore, be central to the shape of our mission since a vital part of our mission is to bear witness to all that God has done in Christ.

The video included a short list of some key elements of this "central act" as found in the four Gospels:

- The fulfilment of Old Testament scriptures
- The incarnation
- The kingdom of God
- The teaching and example of Jesus
- The cross and resurrection
- The gift of the Spirit as empowerment for mission
- The ascension and present reign of Jesus as King

Why and how should all these core elements in the Gospels contribute to our mission thinking and practice – and not just the "Great Commission," as so often emphasized? In other words, how does the Great Commission itself presuppose and draw on the rest of the content of the Gospels?

_____

_____

_____

_____

Which of these distinctive elements in the content of the Gospels do you think have been most neglected in the mission, message, and practice of the church? What effect has such neglect had? Try to be specific, and willing to think honestly of your own church in relation to this question.

_____

_____

_____

_____

Jesus insisted that the Holy Spirit would be essential as "power from on high" for his disciples to be his witnesses (Luke 24:48–49; John 20:21–22; Acts 1:8). Where does that fit into your understanding of mission, and what happens if the work of the Holy Spirit is either ignored or exaggerated?

_____

_____

_____

_____

2. "Look to the future now; it's only just begun."

That familiar line from a Christmas song takes us to Act 6 (Final Judgement) and Act 7 (New Creation) of the Bible drama – final judgement and new creation. In a literal, chronological sense, these events still lie in the future; but they powerfully impact the present.

Some interpretations of mission and evangelism give the impression that it is all simply a matter of "heaven" or "hell" – how to secure a place in one and avoid the other. But is that really all there is to mission?

_____

_____

_____

_____

Based on the video and your reading, how has "the way the Bible ends" in God's new creation shaped your understanding of how our mission fits into God's mission for all creation and all nations?

_____

_____

_____

_____

In what ways is the final judgement part of the gospel? What is "good news" about the final judgement? How might this understanding shape the way we speak or preach about judgement? In what ways does the final judgement make our participation in God's mission significant, crucial, and urgent?

_____

_____

_____

_____

☩ 3. Read Romans 13:11–14 and Colossians 3:4–14

Paul insists that we should live now in light of the future. That is a powerful implication of what we pray in the Lord's Prayer: "Your kingdom come, your will be done on earth as in heaven." If that is what we pray for God to do, then we should live accordingly, or consistently, with what we pray for.

How does Paul's ethical teaching in these passages influence how we connect our daily lives to our sense of mission? In other words, to what extent do we consider that our general everyday duty to *live* and *behave* as obedient followers of Jesus is actually an integral part of our *mission*, since we represent our God and Saviour before the watching world?

_____

_____

_____

_____

Given what the Bible tells us about life in the new creation (Act 7), what kind of behaviour should characterize the way we live now (in Act 5: The Mission of the Church since Pentecost)?

_____

_____

_____

_____

4. So what?

We've come to the end of our overview of the whole Bible as one whole story, as the great drama of God's mission.

In what ways has your view of mission been changed by realizing that God calls all of us to "live in this story" or, in another sense, to "live it out" in our everyday lives, both as individuals and as churches

_____

_____

_____

_____

How does seeing ourselves as participating with God in his mission both keep us *humble* and also give us *confidence* in our own mission efforts? Or, the other way round: What is it about living in God's true story in all its acts, that keeps us from being either *proud* or *pessimistic* in mission?

_____

_____

_____

_____

Digger Deeper Reading

The Great Story and the Great Commission
Read: pages 27–50

Session 4

Gospel-Centred Integral Mission:
Five Marks and Three Spheres of Mission

The main aim of this session is to understand that whatever we do in mission – that is, everything that we consider part of the mission God has given us as individuals and churches – should be held together by *the centrality of the gospel*. In other words, the gospel must be the integrating centre of all our various missional plans and activities. The gospel must be the truth that binds everything else together and justifies the breadth of our mission.

However, to accomplish this, we may need to deepen and broaden our understanding of what the gospel actually is – and we must do this, of course, from the Bible. This is what we will attempt to do in this session.

Brief Starter Question

What does the word "gospel" immediately bring to mind for you?

_____

_____

_____

Video

Watch the video for Session 4.

Discussion

† **1. Read Matthew 28:16–20**

The video emphasized that the lordship of Jesus Christ must be at the centre of the five marks of mission and all three spheres of mission – church, society, and creation.

≡? Why is it important, when applying the Great Commission, to begin with what Jesus claimed about himself before moving on to what he commanded his disciples?

_____

_____

_____

_____

John Stott probably had in mind the opening words of the Great Commission when he linked the lordship of Jesus Christ to mission in the conclusion of his discussion of Philippians 2:9–11.

> There is no greater incentive to world mission than the lordship of Jesus Christ. Mission is neither an impertinent interference in other people's private lives, nor a dispensable option which may be rejected. Mission is an unavoidable conclusion from the universal lordship of Christ.
>
> John Stott, *The Contemporary Christian*, page 98

≡? To what extent would you agree with Stott that mission is "an unavoidable conclusion from the universal lordship of Christ"? Why?

_____

_____

_____

_____

If this statement is true, why is mission so often neglected or treated as optional by so many Christians (and even churches) who would cheerfully affirm, sing, and profess that "Jesus is Lord"?

_____

_____

_____

_____

What things do we often miss or gloss over about the meaning of Christ's lordship?

_____

_____

_____

2. Read Romans 1:1–6 (wherever you see "the Gentiles," please read "the nations" – it's the same word in Greek) and 1 Corinthians 15:1–8

In Romans 1:1, Paul describes himself as "set apart for *the gospel of God*" (NIV).

Look carefully at each phrase in Romans 1:2–4, and make a list of the components of what Paul means by his expression, "the gospel of God."

_____

_____

_____

From 1 Corinthians 15:3–8, add to your list the things "of first importance" that Paul says there by which he defines "the gospel I preached to you" (1 Cor 15:1 NIV).

_____

_____

_____

How does the list you have compiled compare with your earlier answers to what the word "gospel" brought to mind?

_____

_____

_____

_____

I hope that your list included some at least of the following items:

- The Old Testament promise as an essential part of the story (that's what "according to the Scriptures" in 1 Corinthians 15:4 means)
- Jesus's earthly life (his incarnation)
- Jesus being a son of David (What's that about? Paul takes up this concept in Romans 15:12, emphasizing its significance for all nations)
- Jesus death on the cross for our sins
- Jesus resurrection, with multiple eye-witness attestation
- Jesus's exaltation as the Son of God in power (post-resurrection)
- Jesus is both "Christ" (Messiah King) and "our Lord" (a title also given to Caesar in Rome)

Now think back to your brief starter question.

What elements of "the gospel" as defined by Paul were missing from your earlier discussion?

_____

_____

_____

_____

Why do you think these elements were not mentioned in your discussion? Are they usually missing from what Christians these days tend to mean when they think or speak about "the gospel"?

_____

_____

_____

_____

In what ways is "the gospel of God" a bit (or a lot!) bigger than you initially thought?

_____

_____

_____

_____

3. Read Acts 2:22–39

This is Peter "preaching the gospel" on the day of Pentecost (although he doesn't use the word "gospel," the way he concludes his message in verses 38–39 clearly shows that this is good news). Check out and list the elements Peter includes in his message (in a more expanded form) that we also saw Paul include in Romans 1:1–6 and 1 Corinthians 15:1–8.

I hope you noticed at least the following:

- Jesus's amazing earthly life in the power of God (Acts 2:22)

- His death and resurrection (Acts 2:23–24, 32)

- The Old Testament Scriptures (Acts 2:25–28)

- David (Acts 2:25–31)

- Jesus's ascension and exaltation to the right hand of God (Acts 2:33–35)

- Jesus's present status as Lord and Messiah (King, Acts 2:36)
- On the basis of all these facts, Peter calls on the people to repent and be baptized in the name of Jesus Christ, offering forgiveness of sins and the gift of the Holy Spirit as God's guaranteed promise (Acts 2:37–38)

If you have time, you could quickly read **Acts 3:13–26**, where Peter is preaching once again. You will find most of the same elements, including the assertion that Jesus, the Messiah, who is now reigning as Lord, will return when God "restores everything" – a theme that anticipates the very end of the Bible's great story. For Peter, the gospel includes the whole story and its glorious ending in new creation.

If you have time, check out Paul in **Acts 13:16–38,** where you'll see all the same elements, as Paul says, "We tell you the good news" (13:32; the verb is the one usually translated "evangelise").

Why do you think we've spent so much time going through all these extensive examples of "preaching the gospel" by the apostles?

_____

_____

_____

_____

What we're getting at is this: When we use the word "gospel," we tend to think mainly (or only) about personal salvation, focusing on Jesus's death on the cross and receiving forgiveness of our sins. It's "the gospel and me" or, if we're in evangelistic mode, "the gospel and you." It's all very individual. It all sounds like a private transaction between us and God.

All of this is, of course, true: I know that I have been saved and given eternal life through the gospel – praise God!

But when Paul and other apostles speak of the "gospel," they mean the announcement of things that had already happened in recent history, as well as announcing more things that will happen in the future. They were talking about eyewitnessed public events and a future expectation for the world, not just about personal experiences now or up in heaven later. They were telling the world the good news about all that the God of Israel had promised in the Old Testament and then accomplished through Jesus of Nazareth's incarnation, life, death, and resurrection. In addition, through his exaltation as the ascended Lord, Jesus is now the true King and Saviour of the whole world, who will return as its Judge.

The gospel, you see, is not *just* about me getting my sins forgiven because Jesus died for me (although, thank God, it *is* about that, too!). The gospel, according to the New Testament, is the cosmic "good news" declaration of who really rules the world and has saved the world, how and why that is so, and what this means for the future.

After announcing these facts, the apostles call for a *response* to the gospel: "This is what *God* has done (the good news of God); now, this is what *you* must do to benefit from it (so that it becomes good news for you)." This response and result are always:

> • Repent (turn from sin and self to the living God who has done all this)
>
> • Be baptized (which means to enter, by faith, into a new allegiance, a new loyalty, and obedient commitment to Jesus Christ as Lord and King)
>
> • Receive forgiveness of sins and the gift of the Holy Spirit

Now, think back over the texts you have just studied together:

How many of the seven "acts" of the drama of Scripture, which we surveyed in the last two sessions, can you see reflected (either directly mentioned or implied) in the way Peter and Paul think and speak about the "gospel"? Be specific.

_____

_____

_____

_____

How does it expand your understanding of the "gospel" to see that *the entire Bible* is involved in both what the gospel *means* (the facts and the promises that are built into them) and what the gospel *demands* (repentance, faith, and allegiance to Jesus as Lord and King, lived out in obedience in every area of our lives)?

_____

_____

_____

_____

How will this understanding change the way you and your church talk about and use the word "gospel"?

_____

_____

_____

_____

4. Five marks and three spheres

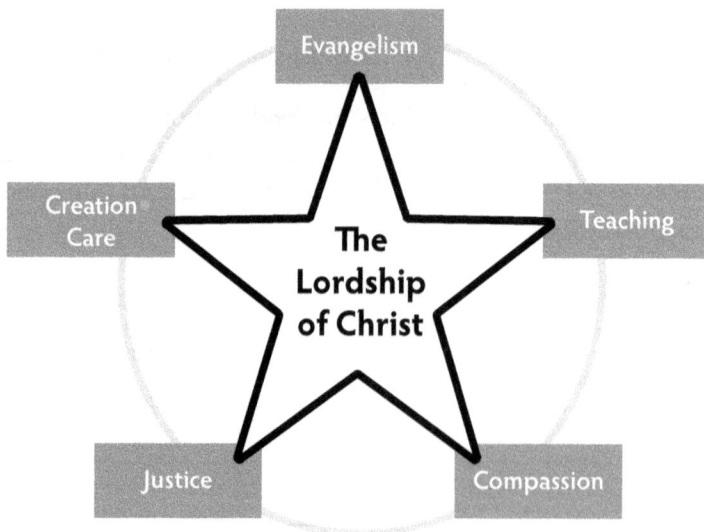

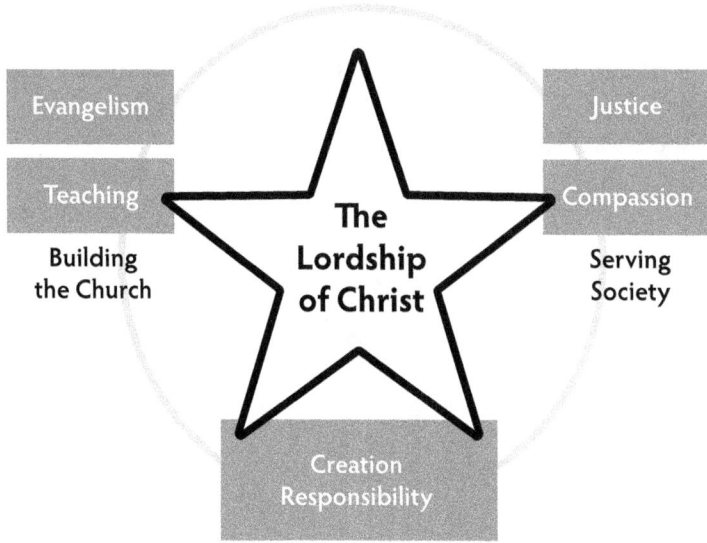

Ruling Over and Caring for Creation

Finally, think back to the video. The diagrams put the lordship of Christ at the centre of the five marks of mission (evangelism, teaching, compassion, justice, and creational responsibility) and also at the centre of the three spheres of mission (building the church, serving society, and responsibly using and caring for creation). I make the point that this is "the centrality of the gospel," which holds everything in mission together.

> Based on the study and discussion above, why is it important that we do not confine the "gospel" to personal forgiveness of sins alone but also include all the ways the New Testament defines the gospel? Remember that Jesus spoke often about "the gospel / good news of *the kingdom of God*." And since Jesus is the king of the kingdom, Paul is essentially saying the same thing in summing up the gospel in the confession that *"Jesus is Lord."*

We naturally see the gospel as essential to evangelism (and, of course, it is). But in what ways do you now see the gospel (in its full biblical sense) as also essential and central to our social action in serving society and caring for creation?

_____

_____

_____

_____

Digging Deeper

The Great Story and the Great Commission
Read: Chapter 4, pages 60–74

Session 5

Building the Church through Evangelism and Teaching

Our main aim in this session is to see how evangelism and teaching were thoroughly integrated in the ministry of Jesus and the early church. In this light, we must consider whether the vision and practice in our own local churches reflect the same dual emphasis.

Brief Starter Question

Would you say that the pastor or minister of your church (or yourself, if that's you) is "doing mission" when they preach on Sundays or lead Bible studies?

_____

_____

_____

_____

Video

Watch the video for Session 5.

Discussion
1. Jesus on mission: Evangelist and teacher

[†] *Read Matthew 4:23 and 9:35.*

[=?] What three verbs does Matthew use to summarize the "everyday work" of Jesus?

_____

_____

_____

_____

Some Christian scholars and theologians believe that the healing miracles of Jesus and his driving out of evil spirits were primarily signs of the in-breaking of God's kingdom. Therefore, these miracles played a unique role in identifying and authenticating Jesus as God's Messiah, meaning that Jesus himself is the "king of God's kingdom." They continued for a while into the book of Acts, but are no longer to be expected in the church and its mission today. However, others would say that, while these miracles were indeed unique in validating Jesus and the kingdom of God, such powerful signs as healings and deliverance ministries have certainly not stopped but should be part of our expectations when God is at work through the missional engagement of his people—especially when the gospel is reaching people for the first time. You may like to discuss this further, but please don't spend too much time on it, and don't let the group fall out over this topic. It's not a key issue for this session. Perhaps you could schedule time for further reflection on this topic on a later occasion.

What is very clear is that, for Jesus, "proclaiming the good news of the kingdom" of God and "teaching in their synagogues" went hand in hand. He was doing both at the same time. One was not more important than the other. Rather, they actually need each other. As Jesus illustrated in the parable of the seed and soils, you can scatter the good seed of the word of God (perhaps symbolizing evangelism), but unless it can takes root in good soil (meaning the soil of people's hearts that is deep and cultivated by good teaching), it won't grow in depth or bear fruit. Evangelism by itself may lead to shallow or short-term growth. Evangelism with good teaching produces transformed lives of godliness and biblical obedience, lives that will bear fruit that lasts.

† Read Mark 3:13–14, Luke 9:1–2, 6, and Luke 10:1–2.

These were the disciples' first mission trips. What instructions were they given? What were they told to pray to God for?

_____

_____

_____

_____

When you compare these episodes from the earthly ministry of Jesus and his disciples with Jesus's commands in the Great Commission (Matt 28:16–20), what similarities and differences do you observe?

_____

_____

_____

2. Paul on mission: Evangelist and teacher

Paul in Philippi

† Read Acts 16:11–15, 25–34.

These are two familiar episodes from Paul's time in Philippi: the first by the river with Lydia and other women; the second in prison with the jailer.

Based on what we've considered in the last session regarding the content of the gospel – including God's promises in the Old Testament Scriptures, what God has accomplished through Jesus, and what God plans to do for the future of creation – what do you think Luke is summarizing when he refers to "Paul's message" (Acts 16:14) and "the word of the Lord" (16:32)? What would such a "message" or "word" have included?

_____

_____

_____

Imagine yourself listening to Paul, both at the riverside and in the jailer's house. Was he doing "evangelism" or "teaching" – or something of both?

_____

_____

_____

_____

Read Philippians 2:5–16

This is the letter Paul wrote to the people who had formed a small church in the city of Philippi – possibly meeting in Lydia's home and probably including the jailer and his family.

How does Paul expect the teaching of the gospel about Jesus (and all he includes in verses 6–11) to impact their life and behaviour?

_____

_____

_____

_____

Notice verse 16. The correct translation should probably be "as you *hold forth* the word of life" (not "hold firmly to"). That is, Paul was expecting the tiny community of believers in Philippi (a Roman colony city, proud of its citizenship and all the dazzle of Roman power), to be verbally sharing "the word of life" (similar to what we would call "evangelism") in the midst of "a warped and crooked generation" and, thereby, to "shine among them like stars in the sky" (Phil 2:15). That implies a combination of living lives that were visibly distinctive and then also, when appropriate, sharing the "word of life" with others in the city.

How would Paul's teaching in the *first part of the chapter* (vs. 1–11) help make that verbal testimony ("the word of life") effective for the gospel (vs. 15–16)?

_____

_____

_____

How might we give more attention to how Paul's teaching in his letters was intended to equip his readers (both then and now) for *more effective mission* in the world around us—and not just for giving us sound doctrine and practical advice for Christian living?

_____

_____

_____

In what ways could we read, teach, and preach the epistles with the assumption and intention that they will strengthen the church's mission in the world?

_____

_____

_____

What difference would such an intentional approach make to your church's preaching (or your own, if you are the preacher)?

_____

_____

_____

Paul in Thessalonica and Athens

†│ *Read Acts 17:1–4, 24–34*

Acts 17 is an interesting chapter because it begins in a Jewish synagogue in
Thessalonica but moves on to a completely pagan public place in Athens. Paul
preaches in both places. In Thessalonica (and later Berea), he speaks to *Jews*
who knew their Scriptures (what we call the Old Testament). In Athens, he
speaks to *Greeks* who knew nothing at all about the Scriptures.

What are the differences and similarities between these two situations?

_____

_____

_____

_____

How does Paul manage to teach significant Old Testament truths in
Athens without actually quoting any Old Testament verses? In what
ways can we do the same when speaking to people who know nothing
of the Bible?

_____

_____

_____

_____

In both places, what (or who) does Paul focus on as he "comes to the
point"? Why is it important that he very intentionally gets to that point
in his teaching?

_____

_____

_____

_____

Paul moved on to Berea (Acts 17:10–12). What did the Jews who listened to him there do (verse 11)? How might that set an example for what we should encourage people to do if they show interest in the gospel message?

_____

_____

_____

_____

† Read 1 Thessalonians 1:8–10 and 2:7–13

Luke tells us that Paul was initially in Thessalonica for only three Sabbaths – which meant he had less than a month with those new believers! But look at how much they had learned in that time, and how Paul had lived out the gospel that he was teaching them.

What does this say about our approach to "evangelism" or "discipling"?

_____

_____

_____

_____

3. Your church on mission: evangelism and teaching

Keeping in mind the New Testament background you've been discussing, spend some time reflecting on your own church (or churches).

How is the gospel (in its fullest sense) integrated into all you do as a church? In what ways is evangelism the heartbeat of your church's life?

_____

_____

_____

_____

How are the evangelistic and teaching/discipling ministries of your church clearly and intentionally connected? (Or do they seem completely unrelated in how they are led and practised?)

_____

_____

_____

_____

In your church's support of overseas world missions, to what extent do your "interests" and support include people, agencies, or projects that are involved in both evangelism/church-planting and teaching/discipling? If they don't, in what ways could you help to strengthen a focus on both.

_____

_____

_____

_____

How can your pastors be encouraged to view their regular ministry of evangelism and teaching as mission, in the sense that it is fully in obedience to the Great Commission, which is not just for foreign missionaries? And if you are the pastor – is that how you see your own commissioning and task?

_____

_____

_____

_____

If your denomination has a theological training arm, such as a seminary or college, how does its work contribute to the church's mission –
that is, fulfilling the second mark of mission and obeying the
Great Commission?

_____

_____

_____

_____

The point of that last question is this. The common assumption is that seminaries or Bible colleges are there to train men and women "for ministry". That is,
they will come out and "do their ministry" in local churches. Paul sees it quite
the other way round. Paul says that Christ has given to the church "the pastors
and teachers *to equip his people for works of service...*" (Eph. 4:11). The work of
ministry and mission in the world belongs to *all* church members, and the job
of pastors is to equip and train them for that task. The congregation does not
"come to church" every Sunday to support the pastor in his or her ministry.
The pastor comes to church every Sunday to equip the people in *their* ministry.

The Cape Town Commitment makes a similar point about theological education
and mission. Read it as a helpful way to conclude this session.

The mission of the Church on earth is to serve the mission of
God, and the mission of theological education is to strengthen
and accompany the mission of the Church. Theological education serves *first* to train those who lead the Church as pastor-
teachers, equipping them to teach the truth of God's Word
with faithfulness, relevance and clarity; and *second*, to equip
all God's people for the missional task of understanding and
relevantly communicating God's truth in every cultural context. Theological education engages in spiritual warfare, as
"we demolish arguments and every pretension that sets itself

up against the knowledge of God, and we take captive every thought to make it obedient to Christ" (2 Corinthians 10:4–5).

Those of us who lead churches and mission agencies need to acknowledge that theological education is intrinsically missional. Those of us who provide theological education need to ensure that it is intentionally missional, since its place within the academy is not an end in itself, but to serve the mission of the Church in the world.

The Cape Town Commitment, IIF.4.

Digging Deeper

The Great Story and the Great Commission
Read: Chapter 5, pages 75–86

Session 6

Serving Society through Compassion and Justice

Brief Starter Question

Given that politics and public life are divided and controversial, how far do you think the church should be involved in social issues?

_____

_____

_____

_____

Video

Watch the video for Session 6.

Discussion
1. The example and teaching of Jesus

| † | *Read Mark 6:6b and Acts 10:38.*

| ≡? | What do these readings say Jesus "went around" doing?

_____

_____

_____

_____

Here is what John Stott says about what these two texts, taken together, say about Jesus:

> There can be no question that words and works went together in his public ministry. True, he was a preacher. He announced the coming of the kingdom of God. But he also demonstrated its arrival by his works of compassion and power . . . There was in his ministry an indissoluble bond between evangelism and compassionate service. He exhibited in action the love of God he was proclaiming . . . So then his words explained his works, and his works dramatized his words. Hearing and seeing, voice and vision, were joined. Each supported the other. For words remain abstract until they are made concrete in deeds of love, while works remain ambiguous until they are interpreted by the proclamation of the gospel. Words without works lack credibility; works without words lack clarity. So Jesus' works made his words visible; his words made his works intelligible.
>
> John Stott, *The Contemporary Christian*, page 245

In light of those verses and John Stott's interpretation, consider these two commonly expressed statements:

"Preach the gospel all the time, *and if necessary use words*" (attributed, probably wrongly, to Francis of Assisi)

"When churches get involved in social action, good works, etc., they quickly get distracted and lose their concern for evangelism."

What dangers do such statements rightly warn us against?

_____

_____

_____

But also, what is wrong or misleading about both of them?

_____

_____

_____

Read Matthew 23:23

According to Jesus, what are the truly important aspects of the Old Testament law? What Old Testament examples can you suggest that would justify these three items? (Hint: Micah 6:8 may help.)

_____

_____

_____

Read Matthew 25:31–46

This passage is like a commentary on Jesus's words in Matthew 23:23. It's as if Jesus is saying, "This is what I mean and why it matters." This is serious stuff – issues of judgement and destiny. It's hard to hear this long passage without feeling uncomfortable.

≡? What challenges do you take from this passage for yourself and your church?

_____

_____

_____

_____

≡? Some argue that since Jesus refers to "the least of these brothers and sisters of mine," the entire passage applies only to how we treat fellow Christians in need, and not to wider society. How might you respond to this suggestion in light of what Jesus says in Matthew 5:43–48?

_____

_____

_____

_____

† *Read Luke 10:25–27 and 15:11–32*

Since these are two very familiar parables of Jesus – the prodigal son and the good Samaritan – you may not need to read through them, but people should have their Bibles open to jog their memories. Notice that the story of the prodigal son, along with the welcoming Father and the angry elder brother, is told in response to what Jesus was facing in Luke 15:1–2.

Here's another wonderful quote from John Stott, comparing both parables and how they address the integration of the evangelistic and social dimensions of our mission. Although this is rather long, it's well worth having the leader or a group member read it aloud or giving some time for everyone to read it quietly.

> If we hold them *[the two parables]* together, they enforce the necessary connection between evangelism and social action. First, in both there is a victim, a man who finds himself in a desperate plight. In the parable of the prodigal son he is the victim of his own sin; in the parable of the good Samaritan

he is the victim of other people's sins . . . Moreover, in the first parable it is personal sin which is described, in the second social sin, namely the evil of public disorder. Both should arouse our compassion. We are concerned both for the sinning and for the sinned against.

Secondly, in both parables there is a rescue – from alienation in a distant land and from violent assault on the road. In the first parable the sinner repents, comes back and is forgiven (it is salvation by faith); in the second the victim can do nothing; he owes his rescue to the charity of the Samaritan (it is a rescue by good works). Thirdly, in both there is a display of love. In the parable of the prodigal son we see the love of God, as the father welcomes the boy home; in the parable of the good Samaritan we see the love of neighbour for neighbour, as the Samaritan binds up the victim's wounds. Moreover, in both cases love triumphs over prejudice. The prodigal is forgiven *although* he deserves no such treatment; the Samaritan takes pity on the robbers' victim, *although* he is an unknown Jew who has no claim on him.

Fourthly, in both parables there is a sub-plot, which dramatizes the alternative to what is being commended. In the parable of the lost son, his elder brother refuses to rejoice in his repentance and return. In the parable of the Samaritan, the priest and Levite refuse to get involved in the battered man's plight. We might even say that those who resist the call to evangelism, and leave people alone in their sins, resemble the elder brother, while those who resist the call to social action, and leave people alone in their sufferings, resemble the priest and the Levite who "passed by on the other side."

Thus each parable emphasizes a vital aspect of Christian discipleship – its beginning when like the prodigal son we come home for salvation, and its continuing when like the good Samaritan we go out in mission. Each of us resembles the prodigal; each of us *should* resemble the Samaritan. First we face our own sins, and then we face the world's sufferings. First we come in and receive mercy, and then we go out and show mercy. Mercy cannot be shown until it has been received; but once it has been received it must be shown to others. Let us

> not divorce what Jesus married. We have all been prodigals; God wants us all to be Samaritans too.
>
> John Stott, *The Contemporary Christian*, pages 346–347, italics original, quoted with permission.

Think about your local church. Is it more committed to seeking and welcoming "prodigal sons and daughters" or to being "good Samaritans"? If there is any tension between those who favour one over the other, what can be done to better balance and integrate both aspects? As John Stott says, "Let us not divorce what Jesus married."

_____

_____

_____

_____

2. The apostle Paul

Open Paul's letter to Titus.

If someone has the NIV 2011 edition (that is, the more recent version), invite them to read out the headings inserted into the main sections of the letter. Can you see the common thread? Titus is a very short letter, yet Paul refers to "what is good" or "good works" no less than seven times (see Titus 1:8, 16; 2:7, 14; 3:1, 8 and emphatically at 3:14). The expression "doing good," which Paul uses several times, was actually a technical term in the Greek and Roman world for various kinds of public benefaction ("benefaction" is the Latin equivalent of one of the Greek words Paul uses). This was not just about "being nice" or generous kindnesses between friends. It meant serving the public good through commendable acts as citizens and neighbours. Even Christian slaves could be "benefactors" (they are included in 3:9–14) – a startling idea!

Paul urges Titus to teach the Christians – old and young, men and women – in Crete (a notorious den of iniquity, as everyone knew – see Titus 1:12) to live lives characterized by visible good deeds. This was not in order that they could get saved. Of course not! Paul is crystal clear that we are not saved by good works (3:5). But those who have been saved by faith must "devote themselves" to doing good (3:8) – for everyone's benefit.

Notice the three times Paul says *"so that . . ."* in the closing lines of Titus 2:5, 2:8, and especially 2:10. What reasons or motivations follow each of these "so that's"? What does Paul see as the results (positive or negative) of sound teaching and doing good works?

_____

_____

_____

_____

In what ways do you think those reasons still apply today in relation to the impact of our private and public lives in commending the gospel?

_____

_____

_____

_____

3. Read this quote from The Cape Town Commitment.

You don't need to read all the references (which are included in the footnote of the text of the Cape Town Commitment itself). But it would be good to have a look at them on your own later. They pack a real challenge!

> All God's people are commanded – by the law and prophets, Psalms and Wisdom, Jesus and Paul, James and John – to reflect the love and justice of God in practical love and justice for the needy.
>   [Exodus 22:21–27; Leviticus 19:33–34; Deuteronomy 10:18–19; 15:7–11; Isaiah 1:16–17; 58:6–9; Amos 5:11–15, 21–24; Psalm 112; Job 31:13–23; Proverbs 14:31; 19:17; 29:7; Matthew 25:31–46; Luke 14:12–14; Galatians 2:10; 2 Corin-

thians 8–9; Romans 15:25–27; 1 Timothy 6:17–19; James 1:27; 2:14–17; 1 John 3:16–18]

Such love for the poor demands that we not only love mercy and deeds of compassion, but also that we do justice through exposing and opposing all that oppresses and exploits the poor. We must not be afraid to denounce evil and injustice wherever they exist. We confess with shame that on this matter we fail to share God's passion, fail to embody God's love, fail to reflect God's character and fail to do God's will. We give ourselves afresh to the promotion of justice, including solidarity and advocacy on behalf of the marginalized and oppressed. We recognize such struggle against evil as a dimension of spiritual warfare that can only be waged through the victory of the cross and resurrection, in the power of the Holy Spirit, and with constant prayer.

The Cape Town Commitment, I.7.c

In what ways does this statement along with the video and the texts you have studied, challenge your view of mission?

_____

_____

_____

What steps will you take, both personally and as a church, to respond?

_____

_____

_____

What could it mean to use a phrase like "gospel-centred holistic mission" as a way of summarizing all that your church does "outside its own walls"? How would that help to integrate all your practical service around the whole biblical gospel and also make sure that the gospel is kept at the centre of all that you do in word and deed?

_____

_____

_____

_____

Digging Deeper

The Great Story and the Great Commission
Read: Chapter 6, pages 87–106

Session 7

Ruling and Caring for Creation

Brief Starter Question

Postage stamps go all over the United Kingdom (or they're supposed to!). Why do they carry an image of King Charles? What is this image "saying"?

_____

_____

_____

_____

Video

Watch the video for Session 7.

There is a lot of material below, and you may decide not to go through all of it in a single session. If that's the case, perhaps you could choose to concentrate on sections 2, 3, 5, and 6, and ask people to read and reflect on the other sections on their own. Alternatively, you could split the study over two sessions.

Why is this section longer than some of the others? Well, probably because you and your group did not need much persuasion that evangelism and discipling are major dimensions of the church's mission. Who doesn't believe that? We hope that most of you also now have a good grasp of why issues involving practical social compassion and justice must be addressed in the light of the biblical gospel and are, therefore, part of our integrated and holistic mission. However, for many Christians, it's much harder to see how and why creation itself has an important place within our missional thinking and practice. Therefore, we need to spend a bit more time thinking through this topic in the light of the Bible. And even then, not everyone will be persuaded.

This may be a session where people disagree. Sadly, this issue of creation care has become divisive and politicized among Christians in some countries. Please try to stay focused on the biblical material and its implications, and avoid getting drawn into political or "culture war" arguments.

Discussion
1. Creation – Who cares?

Does God really care about the earth itself? Judging from much Christian worship and discussion, especially around the topic of mission, it is clear that God cares for *people*. After all, God demonstrated just how much he loves and cares for people by sending Jesus to die on the cross for our salvation. But the earth? The animals, birds, fish, and insects? The trees and plants? The rivers, oceans, mountains, and forests? Does God care about them – love them, even?

Read these passages aloud one after the other:

† Psalm 65:9–13

Psalm 104:10–30

Psalm 145:8–9, 15–17

Matthew 6:25–27

Matthew 10:29

What is the dominant picture of God in relation to creation that you gain from these verses?

_____

_____

_____

_____

How does that affect the way you think and feel about the earth, considering that our thoughts should, in some way, reflect God's own thoughts?

_____

_____

_____

_____

It might be appropriate just to pause and give a few moments for prayer, confessing to God that our thoughts about the creation around us often seem very far from God's own.

2. Creation – Who rules and how?

Read Genesis 1:26–28 and 2:15

What is the main reason God created human beings in his own image?

_____

_____

_____

_____

How would you explain what it means, in practice, for us to act as God's image in relation to the earth and its creatures?

_____

_____

_____

_____

In the video, I said that the balancing verbs in Genesis 1 ("rule over") and Genesis 2 ("work" or "serve," and "keep") give humans the dual role of being "kings and priests" on earth on God's behalf. Some people argue that the language of kingship (ruling) is to blame for the way human beings cruelly exploit and abuse the earth and the non-human creation. But is that fair?

† *Read Psalm 8*

Here's a quote from Dave Bookless's excellent book, *Planetwise*:

> God not only cares for human beings, he has also given us a role that is far more than we deserve . . .
>
> > You made him a little lower than the heavenly
> > beings
> > And crowned him with glory and honour.
> > You have made him ruler over the works of your
> > hands;
> > You put everything under his feet. (Psalm 8:6)
>
> Humans have a place in creation that comes not by right but as a gift from God. The imagery in Psalm 8:5–6 is that of royalty: God has crowned us kings and queens, sitting on a throne with the world symbolically under our feet. Being 'under our feet' is not about trampling down, but symbolic of reflecting God's just and righteous royal authority over all creation.
>
> *Planetwise: Dare to Care for God's World* (IVP, 2008), pages 32–33

The way we behave as kings within creation should reflect the way God exercises his own kingship. So, what kind of king is God?

| † | *Read Psalm 145:8–17*

The whole Psalm is addressed to "My God the King" (Ps 145:1) and speaks of his glorious kingdom. But what kind of king is described in verse 9? Notice how verse 9 extends the great truth of verse 8 (quoting Exodus 34:6) from humans to "all he has made."

The Psalm tells us that God the King is good and compassionate towards "all he has made" (*all his works*, not just people) and indeed "loving to all he has made" (verse 17, as a more likely translation than "faithful in all he does"). In the light of that, how does God's example challenge the way we, who are created in God's image, reflect *God's* kingship on earth?

_____

_____

_____

_____

3. Whose earth is it anyway?

Read aloud, one after the other, Deuteronomy 10:14, Psalm 24:1, Psalm 50:10–11, and Psalm 115:16

If the earth is God's property, which has been gifted or entrusted to us, how does that affect the way we use and enjoy its resources?

_____

_____

_____

_____

In Israel, the people were to think of their land in the same way that these texts speak of the whole earth. In other words, the land of Canaan was given to them by God as their possession, but God remained the ultimate owner of this land. God was the true landlord, and they were his tenants – accountable to him for everything they did on and with the land, including its animals and crops. This foundational principle is expressed in Leviticus 25, which deals with down-to-earth economic arrangements in matters relating to land, debt, mortgaging, and redemption of loans.

> The land must not be sold permanently, because the land is mine and you reside in my land as foreigners and strangers. Throughout the land that you hold as a possession, you must provide for the redemption of the land. (Lev 25:23–24 NIV)

If you have time, skim through the following texts to see some very practical outworkings of this principle in relation to domestic animals, wild birds, sanitation, and farm produce (or you could read these passages later on your own): Deuteronomy 22:1–4, 6–7; 23:12–14; 24:19–22. When I read these verses, it reminds me of a friend in India who, as a Hindu, had started reading the Bible for the very first time, marvelling at this God he was encountering there. "I never knew such a God existed," he exclaimed to me, as he told me how he had come to Christian faith. "This God thinks of everything!" was his amazement as he read through the books of Leviticus and Deuteronomy. Indeed he does – and that extends to very practical care for what we now call "the environment."

Paul quotes Psalm 24:1 – "The earth is the Lord's" – in 1 Corinthians 10:26. The "Lord" clearly refers to Jesus Christ, as in the rest of the chapter. *Christ* is the creator, sustainer, and redeemer of the whole creation, including our broken, sin-soaked earth. This is the mind-boggling scale of what Paul affirms about Christ in Colossians. As you read the passage below, notice how many times Paul refers to "all things" and "in heaven and on the earth," obviously referring to the whole of creation, including the earth we live on.

† *Read Colossians 1:15–20. Read it aloud and slowly.*

Now read the extract below from *The Cape Town Commitment* (which was also quoted in the video).

> The earth is created, sustained and redeemed by Christ. We cannot claim to love God while abusing what belongs to Christ by right of creation, redemption and inheritance. We [as Christians] care for the earth and responsibly use its abundant resources, not according to the rationale of the secular

world, but for the Lord's sake. If Jesus is Lord of all the earth, we cannot separate our relationship to Christ from how we act in relation to the earth. For to proclaim the gospel that says "Jesus is Lord" is to proclaim the gospel that includes the earth, since Christ's Lordship is over all creation.

The Cape Town Commitment, I.7a

In light of the Colossians reading and the quoted extract, how might we think differently about what it means to claim that *we love God* in the way we treat *God's property* – remembering that all God's creation belongs to Christ?

_____

_____

_____

_____

4. Who's to blame? Is there hope?

"Cursed is the ground because of you," said God to Adam, after Adam and Eve had distrusted God's goodness, disregarded his authority, and disobeyed his commands (Gen 3:17 NIV). Our relationship with our physical environment – just like our relationships with God and one another – is twisted and spoiled. We suffer, and creation suffers because of our actions. The Bible recognizes the very close intertwining of human sin and creational devastation and suffering. Here are just two examples of this:

Read Hosea 4:1–3

Hosea describes a whole culture that has forgotten God, resulting in not just appalling *social* consequences but also devastating *environmental* consequences that affect land, sea, and sky. Hosea could have been talking about our world today.

|t| *Read Habakkuk 2:17*

This verse is part of a whole list of accusations ("woes") against the Babylonian Empire, specifically under Nebuchadnezzar and his warmongering aggression. "Lebanon" refers to the great forests of cedars, cut down for war-machines. The accusation sounds very modern: "violence" and "destruction" not just of human beings but also of forests, animals, land, and cities – the whole environment.

How seriously do you and your church take the various environmental crises in our world today, especially the global threat of climate breakdown and its impacts on so many people, especially the poor?

_____

_____

_____

_____

But is there hope? Hope is found only in God's covenant promise, the covenant he made through Noah, with all life on earth.

|t| *Read Genesis 8:20–22 and 9:8–17*

Notice the frequent references to "every living creature" and "all life" on earth. We face a practical challenge in responding to these biblical teachings.

On the one hand, we live on an earth where God's *curse* is evident, where the ecological crisis is aggravated by human folly, sin, greed, violence, and exploitation. What can we do, even in small ways, to counteract these issues?

_____

_____

_____

_____

On the other hand, we also live on an earth where God's *covenant* still sustains all of creation. How can we give practical expression to our faith in this truth?

_____

_____

_____

_____

5. Does the earth have a future?

Read Isaiah 65:17–25

What future for the earth does God promise in this wonderful vision?

_____

_____

_____

_____

Some people may view this vision as merely "symbolic" or "material-istic." But in the light of what we've seen of God's care for all life on earth – both human and non-human – how should we interpret this vision? What truth is it telling us about God's ultimate plan for "heaven and earth"?

_____

_____

_____

_____

What does verse 25 tell you about God's vision for environmental peace and harmony?

_____

_____

_____

_____

Read 2 Peter 3:3–13

Some people take verses 10 and 12 literally, and then dismiss creation care as a pointless waste of time: "If it's all going to be burned up in the end, why should we care for it now?" However, they probably don't take that same attitude with regard to their own bodies in anticipation of possible future cremation. Would you trust a doctor who said something like that if you go to them with some serious illness: "Well you're going to die and be all burnt up some day, so why should I waste time caring for you now?" So why take that attitude to creation? Paul links creation and our bodies together powerfully in Romans 8:18–23 – with solid redemptive hope for both.

Let's take a closer look at Peter's comparison between the flood and the final judgement.

What and who were "destroyed" in the "waters" of the flood (2 Pet 3:6)?

_____

_____

_____

_____

What and who will be destroyed in the "fire" of "judgement" (2 Pet 3:7)?

_____

_____

_____

_____

Peter uses the stereotypical language of apocalyptic judgement to show that the present creation will be purged or cleansed of sin, evil, and "the ungodly" (2 Pet 3:7). That's what the fire will do. He is not saying that the earth will be obliterated entirely (any more than the earth itself was obliterated in the flood). It will be all the sin and evil that will be burnt away, leaving the earth itself renewed and cleansed as the dwelling place for God and his people.

In verse 13, how does Peter describe the "end result" of the final judgement?

_____

_____

_____

What Old Testament scripture do his words "a new heaven and a new earth" bring to mind? (Hint: We just read it above.)

_____

_____

_____

Read Revelation 21:1–8

This passage is John's interpretation and expansion of Isaiah's vision of God's new creation, in which God will dwell with us (the ultimate "Immanuel" fulfilment). Please note carefully that the Bible does not end with us *going up* to heaven. What John sees in his climactic great vision is God, heaven, and the city of God, *coming down* to earth – an earth that is now renewed and cleansed of all evil, fit for God's own dwelling at last.

The redeemed from all nations will then serve God as kings and priests (Rev 22:3, 5), just as God intended from the beginning.

Where will we be doing that? (Rev 5:10).

_____

_____

_____

How radical is it to realize that the Bible sees our ultimate future not as "up in heaven" but "here on earth" – a cleansed, redeemed, and renewed earth? Why does so much popular Christianity (and some of the things we sing in popular hymns and songs) keep on perpetuating the idea that we will some day all go off somewhere else ("up", or "home"), when the Bible clearly teaches that it is God who will come here to cleanse and renew his whole creation and *dwell with us* forever?

_____

_____

_____

_____

6. What next?

If this very rapid survey of just a tiny fraction of what the Bible has to say about God, creation, and about our relationship with the earth (past, present, and future) has changed or challenged your thinking, share your thoughts and discuss what difference this should make in your personal life. Discuss how might this influence your church community. This could be a significant part of a "missional audit" that your church could conduct (see Session 8 and the section on "Further Resources").

Digging Deeper

The Great Story and the Great Commission
Read: Chapter 7, pages 107–111, 124–127
Read: Chapter 8, pages 128–140

Session 8

Mission and the Local Church

Video

Watch the video for Session 8.

The Bible study element of this session is a bit shorter, so please allow plenty of time to discuss the important "So what?" questions in section 3. It is crucial to finish this course with some practical resolutions and actions as a result of working through the whole journey of "understanding mission" in terms of its biblical foundations.

Discussion

"If everything is mission, nothing is mission."

Have you heard that opinion? It expresses the fear that some people have – that if we broaden our definition of mission to include a wide range of activities (almost everything a church does), we may lose the sense of mission as a very specific activity of the church, especially in evangelistic outreach and in sending out and supporting international, cross-cultural mission partners. Mission ought to mean something in particular, not just everything in general – that's the idea.

We hope that the strong emphasis on those particular aspects of mission (evangelism and international mission) – in the videos, and in earlier sessions of this Study Guide – will address this concern. As we have already stressed, gospel-centred integral mission *must* include evangelistic commitment, both at home and abroad. However, what we are saying here is that such evangelistic commitment is not all there is to mission, but rather that *mission encompasses all that God sends the church into the world to do.* It might be better to say, "if everything is mission, then everything is mission!" –but not all in the same way or the same time.

One way to get our heads around this – as suggested by the well-known mission theologian Lesslie Newbigin – is to recognize that while all church activities should have a missional *dimension,* some activities may have a specific missional *intention.*

We have seen that God's people exist in the world *for the sake of God's mission.* The church serves this mission of God, aligning ourselves with what God has done, is doing, and plans to do for the world. We are God's partners, co-workers with God as Paul says. That is the enormous privilege, blessing and responsibility of being the people whom God has redeemed and called to himself and to his service.

For this reason, there should be a missional *dimension* to all of a church's life and activities. Everything a church does should be connected, or contribute in some way, to the reason for its existence. Gathering for worship, to praise God and hear his word, strengthens our faith and courage for our life and witness in the world. Fellowship with other believers does the same. All teaching and pastoring is intended "to equip the saints for the work of ministry" (Eph 4:12 NRSV) – which is another way of saying, to strengthen us in God's service and mission. Praying together (on Sundays or midweek) for the world is in itself a participation in God's mission. All the arrangements and logistics and money that go into the life of a church should be justified on the basis of the extent to which they help the church to *be* what it is called to be – God's people for God's mission in God's world. There should be a thoughtful missional *dimension* to all that a church does, in the sense that the leaders and people have a clear sense of "what we are here for" which gives coherence and significance to the whole life of the church.

But within this overall life of the church, there will also be decisions and actions that have a specific missional *intention.* This may include evangelistic events, outreach initiatives, practical involvement in the community as Christian citizens, programmes to serve the needy in the neighbourhood, involvement in overseas mission through financial support and prayer, world mission

Sundays, and the calling, sending, and supporting of mission partners when God so leads. These are just a few examples of intentional missional planning and action. All of them, including but not confined to evangelism of course, should be clearly gospel-centred and gospel-motivated, bearing witness to what God has done in Christ and the light and hope that brings into a world full of darkness and despair

Here are two short Bible studies that illustrate both aspects of mission.

1. Missional dimension of a church's life

$\boxed{\dagger}$ *Read Hebrews 13:1–16*

As the writer concludes his letter, take note of the things he urges his readers to keep on practising in their life together.

I noticed the following:

- Mutual love (Heb 13:1)

- Practical compassion, hospitality, and care for the needy (Heb 13:2–3)

- Sexual purity (Heb 13:4)

- Financial contentment (Heb 13:5–6)

- The spoken word, probably referring to initial evangelism and church planting (Heb 13:7)

- Resisting false teaching and replacing it with good teaching, as emphasized throughout the letter (Heb 13:9–11)

- Willing identification with Jesus in social disgrace (Heb 13:12–13)

- Public worship and praise (Heb 13:15)

- Persevering in doing good works and generosity (Heb 13:16)

While the writer of Hebrews was almost certainly not thinking about "mission" in the sense that we understand it today, how might the dimensions of church life listed above contribute to the church's effectiveness in serving God's missional purpose in its surroundings?

_____

_____

_____

_____

_____

Which of these marks of the church are evident in the life of your church? What *gaps* do you notice? What challenge does this present for the "*missional dimension*" of all that goes on in your church?

_____

_____

_____

_____

_____

Make a quick list of all the regular activities of your church. What are some ways in which each of these activities is connected to, or contributes to, the reason your church exists for the sake of God's kingdom and mission in your context?

_____

_____

_____

_____

_____

2. Missional intention in a church's life

[†] *Read 3 John 5–8*

This short letter was written to a local church leader named Gaius, probably in the region of Ephesus. The writer ("the elder") expresses his delight at the news that Gaius has continued to be faithful to the truth (3 John 3–4). He then commends him for being "faithful in what you are doing for the brothers and sisters, even though they are strangers to you" (3 John 5 NIV). These "brothers and sisters" were probably itinerant Christian travellers around the eastern Mediterranean, and we know something about them from the New Testament, particularly Paul's letters. Some of them, like Paul, were evangelists and church planters, while others – like Apollos – brought apostolic teaching. Remember, the New Testament had not yet been written! Others carried letters or commendations from one church to another. Some would have needed the hospitality of a church where they were unknown in order to continue their travels to other places, taking the gospel. These people share some similarities with modern cross-cultural missionaries.

Clearly, Gaius and his church had been very *intentional* in what they were doing for these men and women – they were participating in mission beyond their own local city. Although they were a *local* church, they saw themselves as part of a wider *overseas* team (even though there was just one "sea" to cross "over" at that time – the Mediterranean), and in that team they were all "work[ing] together for the truth" (3 John 8 NIV).

[†] *Look carefully at verses 6, 7, and 8.*

Sending (verse 6). The word translated "send them on their way" meant a lot more than just waving them goodbye on the ship. It was a technical term for providing all that was necessary for safe travel: food, money, companions, letters of commendation, and so on. If your church is involved in this kind of "sending" of mission partners, what does it mean to do so "in a manner that honours God"? If it was Jesus himself that you were sending as a missionary, what would you do for him? Would 3 John 6 be a good motto for your world mission committee?

Going (verse 7). What was the motivation of those who were travelling, and what did that involve in practice?

_____

_____

_____

Supporting (verse 8). "We ought" is a rather weak translation. The phrase really means "We have an obligation; we are duty bound" In addition, "show hospitality" meant far more than offering a cup of tea and a bed for the night. In the Greek and Roman world of the day, travellers needed safety and substantial provisions. What priority does your church give to ensuring adequate support for the kind of people described in verse 7? Do you consider the practical and specific needs of those serving God in places far from home and sensitively enquire about how you can help to meet them?

_____

_____

_____

Do each of these three words in three verses reflect something in the life of your church? What might you need to do to be more like Gaius and his friends?

_____

_____

_____

_____

3. A missional audit

Think back over the five marks of mission (evangelism, teaching, compassion, justice, creational responsibility) and the three spheres of mission (building the church, serving society, godly use and care of creation). Use these as a "template" to assess your church's life, work, ministry, and mission. If you are part of the leadership of your church, would you consider conducting a "missional audit"? Here are some questions that could be part of that. They may stimulate you to ask other questions and probe more deeply into the missional "health" (or otherwise) of your church.

Is your church active in each those five marks and three spheres, in various ways--in word and deed, in preaching and teaching, in budgeting, in time given, in information received and shared, in planned activities or projects, in personal or financial support) While it is not necessary (or even possible or advisable) that every mark or sphere should receive exactly the same amount of time or staff or money or anything, it is important that every dimension of mission receives some consideration and engagement. Pay attention to what may easily get overlooked or swamped out.

_____

_____

_____

_____

Is attention being given not only to the church's immediate neighbourhood – with its specific demographic, social, and spiritual needs – but also to the wider world, the global church, and international cross-cultural mission, so that your local church may "work together for the truth" (3 John 8) within the worldwide body of Christ?

_____

_____

_____

If there are serious gaps in any of these areas, what can you do to address these?

_____

_____

_____

Every church is different and so are all the contexts in which God has placed each community of believers. What works well in one place might be impossible or unwise in another. We should think about where our specific priorities may lie, and these will vary depending on all the aspects of our context – social, economic, political, cultural, ethnic, religious, etc etc. However, it is important to pay attention to any blind spots or neglected areas and make plans to rectify them. A planned "missional audit" could be a good way to start.

Is there a consciously missional *dimension* to the whole life of your church in all its varied modes and activities?

_____

_____

_____

And are there strategically planned missional *intentions* being put into practice that involve not just a few over-loaded enthusiasts, but the whole church body?

_____

_____

_____

_____

Finally

Behind both missional dimensions and missional intentions lies a *missional mindset.* How will you *"think missionally"* about your church life? This will mean continually asking the question, "How does this or that part of what we do as a church connect with, or contribute to, our reason for being here as God's people in this place for God's purposes?"

_____

_____

_____

_____

A truly missional church is one that keeps on asking, not just, "What shall we *do next*?" but also, "*What are we here for?*"

_____

_____

_____

_____

Thank you for persevering through this study course. I hope it has left you with an enlarged understanding from the Bible of what "mission" ought to mean (even if the word itself isn't in the Bible!). And I hope it has led to some concrete resolutions and plans that will impact the life of your church in the days and years ahead.

May the Lord bless his word and glorify the Lord Jesus Christ in his people.

Digging Deeper

The Great Story and the Great Commission
Read: Chapter 9, pages 141–152

Further Resources

We hope this course has been helpful in helping you grasp the whole topic of "mission" from a broad biblical point of view. Eventually, we hope to produce additional materials and point people to other study courses and resources. So, if any individuals in your group, or perhaps the leadership of your church, are motivated to take their interest in mission further, do keep an eye on the Understanding Mission website for further developments.

As we mentioned at the beginning, this eight-session course only scratches the surface of a subject that has occupied the hearts and minds of God's people around the world for many centuries – not to mention the many books written on this topic.

Well, actually, on second thoughts, let's mention some books!

Here are some suggestions for further reading for those who want to dig even deeper. The selection mostly includes books that reflect the biblical foundations for mission that this course has explored. But it also includes titles that provide a historical survey of the global church's understanding and practice of mission through the ages and today. It also includes authors whose names may not be familiar to Western ears.

It is very important that those of us who live in Western countries do not imagine that we are "the sending church" and that everywhere else is "the mission field." That paradigm passed its sell-by date a long time ago (and was never really true anyway). Today, the global church is far larger in the continents of Africa, Asia, and Latin America (sometimes called the "Global South" or the "Majority World") than in the West. The clue is in the name – the *majority* (at least 70 percent) of all those who call themselves Christians of any sort live in the "non-Western" parts of the world.

World mission reflects this reality. Mission is from everywhere to everywhere, and we in the West must listen to the experiences and voices of sisters and brothers from parts of the world where the church is often growing amazingly fast in spite of suffering, poverty, and persecution. That is the "world" in which Langham Partnership serves, walking alongside Christian churches, leaders, and institutions, primarily in the Majority World. One of the Langham programmes is "Langham Literature," and one of its key ministries is publishing books by Majority-World Christians – amplifying their voice in their own world and for the benefit of the Western church. You will find below a number of titles published by Langham. And you can find even more titles – a full and colourful catalogue – on the Langham Literature website: https://langhampublishing.org/.

General books on mission

There are hundreds of books on mission! However, here are some titles that people have found helpful and reasonably accessible.

Christopher J. H. Wright, *The Mission of God: Unlocking the Bible's Grand Narrative* (IVP, 2006). This is a very broad survey of major biblical themes that provide the theological foundation for our mission by seeing the whole Bible as the record and product of God's mission. Note: a 2nd edition (fully revised, updated, and expanded) will be published in October 2025.

Christopher J. H. Wright, *The Mission of God's People: A Biblical Theology of the Church's Mission* (Zondervan, 2010). This book is more popular and accessible than the title listed above. It asks, "If that is the mission of God in the whole Bible, then what is the mission of the church? What kind of people does God call us to be, according to both the Old and New Testaments?"

Michael W. Goheen, *Introducing Christian Mission Today: Scripture, History and Issues* (IVP, 2014). This is a textbook on mission, which includes several major sections: Biblical and Theological; Historical and Contemporary; and Current Issues. It is remarkably comprehensive and informative. A book to study over time!

John Stott and Christopher J. H. Wright, *Christian Mission in the Modern World* (IVP, updated and expanded edition, 2015). This small classic by John Stott was first published in 1975. It explores five "big words": Mission, Evangelism, Dialogue, Salvation, and Conversion. The updated edition includes additional material and reflections by Chris Wright.

Sessions 1–3: Reading the whole Bible as one great story of God's mission

Craig Bartholomew and Michael Goheen, *The Drama of Scripture: Finding Our Place in the Biblical Story* (3rd edition, Baker, 2024). This is a superb telling of the whole Bible story, with its implications for our understanding of the mission of God himself, and our place within it.

Bernardo Cho, *The Plot of Salvation: Divine Presence, Human Vocation, and Cosmic Redemption* (Langham Global Library, 2022). This book is based on twenty sermons preached by Bernardo Cho, a Brazilian pastor and Langham Scholar, to help his congregation navigate through the story of the entire Bible. The book gets you from Genesis to Revelation, with a wealth of discoveries en route.

Michael Goheen, *A Light to the Nations: The Missional Church and the Biblical Story* (Baker, 2011). This is a more academic study but is accessible to theological students and pastors. It explores the doctrine of the church (ecclesiology) in relation to the whole biblical narrative and the mission God has for his people throughout.

Sessions 4 and 5: Evangelism and teaching/discipling

David E. Bjork, *Every Believer a Disciple! Joining in God's Mission* (Langham Global Library, 2015). In recent decades, the growth of Christianity has been remarkable, but has this been growth with depth? Are our communities of faith – our churches – creating and nurturing deeply committed followers of Jesus? This book, written by an author who has lived and taught in Africa for many years, seeks to ensure that church planting leads to the development of growing and maturing disciples.

Ermias Mamo, *The Maturing Church: An Integrated Approach to Contextualization, Discipleship and Mission* (Langham Global Library, 2017). In this book, an Ethiopian church leader and theological teacher explores what effective discipleship looks like in his context and offers valuable lessons for the wider church.

Hikmat Kashouh, *Following Jesus in Turbulent Times: Disciple-Making in the Arab World* (Langham Global Library, 2018). Hikmat Kashouh, a Langham Scholar, pastors the Resurrection Church in Beirut, Lebanon, which God has built up under his leadership with several thousand new believers in multiple church hubs. Many of these believers are Syrian refugees, for whom Hikmat has developed pathways to mature discipleship and leadership of others. The book offers valuable insights into practical and effective ways to enable healthy church growth.

Dave Jensen, *Mission* (Reach Australia, 2023). This resource is aimed at helping a local church to think through its evangelistic strategy within its own neighbourhood. It provides both biblical motivation and practical advice. You can freely access it at: https://reachaustralia.com.au/mission-ebook/

Timothy Keller, *Center Church: Doing Balanced, Gospel-Centered Ministry in Your City* (Zondervan, 2012). This is an influential book by the renowned church leader and author Tim Keller. Many churches in different parts of the world have found this book both gospel-centred and inspiring for devising practical evangelistic and discipleship strategies in their own cities.

Grove Books. https://grovebooks.co.uk/. These short booklets are packed with solid content that's easy to read, while also combining sound biblical thinking with practical help and the benefit of experience. Check out the many titles in the Discipleship Series and the Mission and Evangelism Series.

Session 6: Compassion and justice

There are so many books on gospel-centred holistic or integral mission that choosing just a few is very difficult. But here are some titles that we recommend:

Rupen Das, *Compassion and the Mission of God: Revealing the Invisible Kingdom* (Langham Global Library, 2016). This book traces God's compassion as revealed in the Old and New Testaments, exploring the expression and impact of compassion in the early church through its actions and teachings as part of its witness. It provides an excellent biblical and theological foundation for anyone involved or interested in the ministries of social justice, relief, development, and compassion.

Tim Monger, *Transforming Church: Participating in God's Mission through Community Development* (Langham Global Library, 2023). Tim Monger draws on over a decade of experience working in integral mission alongside local congregations in East Africa. In this book, he explores the theological and biblical foundations for integral mission alongside its practical realities and casts a vision for what can be achieved when the church serves society in ways that are biblically grounded, culturally appropriate, and practically relevant.

Graham Joseph Hill (editor), *Relentless Love: Living out Integral Mission to Combat Poverty, Injustice and Conflict* (Langham Global Library, 2020). In this collection of essays, Christians from across the globe reflect on the church's role in alleviating suffering and developing transformed communities. This book ignites a biblical passion for integrating justice and proclamation, witness and social concern, evangelism and community transformation.

Tim Chester, *Good News to the Poor: Social Involvement and the Gospel* (Crossway, 2013). This book offers biblical support for social involvement and its integral relationship with evangelistic witness, while also speaking in practical terms about what local churches can do.

Michael Rhodes, *Just Discipleship: Biblical Justice in an Unjust World* (IVP, 2023). Justice is one of the biggest words in the Bible – applied both to God himself and to what God demands of us. But what does it mean, and why is it so controversial? Rhodes offers provides a rich survey of biblical truth and teaching, along with practical wisdom that can be applied in the lives of individual Christians and churches.

Session 7: Responsible use and care of creation

Dave Bookless, *Planetwise: Dare to Care for God's World* (IVP, 2008). Bookless offers a thorough biblical understanding of the importance of God's creation, along with practical recommendations for "living it out" – in the areas of discipleship, worship, lifestyle and mission, "as if creation matters."

Dave Bookless, *God Doesn't Do Waste: Redeeming the Whole of Life* (IVP, 2010). In this follow-up to *Planetwise*, Bookless shares the remarkable and inspiring story of A Rocha in the UK and his family's personal journey in creation care.

Douglas Moo and Jonathan Moo, *Creation Care: A Biblical Theology of the Natural World* (Zondervan, 2018). This accessible book is filled with solid biblical teaching and wise discussion of serious contemporary issues.

R. J. (Sam) Berry, *John Stott on Creation Care* (IVP, 2021). This marvellous collection of quotes from the whole range of John Stott's writings over several decades shows not only his love for nature but also his strong biblical and theological convictions about the need to include creation in the church's understanding of discipleship and mission.

Jonathan Moo and Robert White, *Let Creation Rejoice: Biblical Hope and Ecological Crisis* (IVP, 2014). This book combines helpful explanations of the science behind change and its impacts, along with thorough biblical reflection on these issues. It is not alarmist but fosters hope and action, based on solid biblical teaching about creation and the new creation.

Paul Kunert, *Jesus Died to Save the Planet* (LICC, 2024). This is a short booklet, but it packs a powerful message. Kunert reclaims the foundational truth that the gospel is good news for the whole of creation. The apostle Paul taught the full redemptive reach of Jesus's sacrifice, and we need to embrace the full, holistic scope of the gospel – living in line with the truth that Jesus is King of all things and came to save all he has made.

Session 8 : Mission and the local church

Neil Hudson, *Imagine Church: Releasing Whole-Life Disciples* (IVP, 2012). This is one of several excellent resources from the London Institute for Contemporary Christianity. https://licc.org.uk/. This book encourages churches to move from a purely "attractional" mindset (inviting people to church to hear the gospel) to become "inside-out" – focusing on where most people spend most of their time in their daily lives and how they can live positively and missionally in those places. It is full of practical wisdom, case studies, and suggestions.

Mark Greene, *The Great Divide* (LICC, 2010; updated 2024). This small but powerful book exposes the terrible damage that the "secular-sacred divide" has caused in the church, where most Christians imagine that God is only interested in some parts of their lives and that only the few Christians called to so-called full-time ministry are doing "God's work." Overcoming this dichotomized thinking is a crucial step in helping a church to fully engage in God's mission in the world.

Mark Greene and Ian Shaw (editors), *Whole-Life Mission for the Whole Church: Overcoming the Sacred-Secular Divide through Theological Education* (Langham Global Library, 2021). Building on the insights of *The Great Divide*, this book is primarily for those involved in theological education. However, it also has value for thoughtful church leaders seeking to address the "divide" in the minds of their own congregations.

Michael Goheen and Jim Mullins, *The Symphony of Mission: Playing Your Part in God's Work in the World* (Baker, 2019). Through reflecting on church life in the USA, this warm and deeply personal book has wide value as it explores how local churches and their members can develop a missional mindset that leads to practical actions that serve the kingdom of God in the midst of everyday life.

Darrell Cosden, *The Heavenly Good of Earthly Work* (Paternoster and Hendrickson, 2006). This excellent and highly readable short theology of work helps Christians to value all honest work as a way to serve God and others in this life and in creation. It also helps them understand the significance of our work in God's mission and the Bible's vision of the new creation.

Resources for a church undertaking a "mission audit"

If your church does decide to follow up on the suggestion in Session 8 to conduct a "missional audit" – that is, to explore whether your church's life and ministry includes some intentional missional engagement in the five marks of mission and three spheres of mission – one of the first challenges you may face is this: Where can we find information about these topics? What resources are available? Who should we connect with?

Here are a few suggestions that you may wish to explore. The Understanding Mission website provides more ideas and includes an interactive space for people to share their own experiences, knowledge, and connections for the benefit of others.

On evangelism and global mission

Lausanne Movement (and its multiple Issue Networks)
https://lausanne.org/

Global Connections
https://globalconnections.org.uk/

On teaching and discipling

LICC
https://licc.org.uk/

Langham Partnership
https://langham.org/

Increase Association
https://increaseassociation.org/

Scholar Leaders
https://scholarleaders.org/

On Compassion ministries

Tear Fund
https://tearfund.org/

Micah Global
https://micahglobal.org/

On Justice ministries

International Justice Mission
https://ijm.org/

Christian Solidarity Worldwide
https://csw.org.uk/

Christians Against Poverty
https://capuk.org/

On Creation Care

A Rocha
https://arocha.org.uk/

Evangelical Environmental Network
https://creationcare.org/

Lausanne Creation Care Network
https://lausanne.org/network/creation-care

EXPAND YOUR VISION FOR MISSION

Both this study guide and the Understanding Mission online course are based on and complement the 2024 Christianity Today Book of the Year in Missions – *The Great Story and the Great Commission* (Baker 2023).

As highlighted throughout this study guide, if you wish to dig deeper into understanding mission then this volume is a perfect companion.

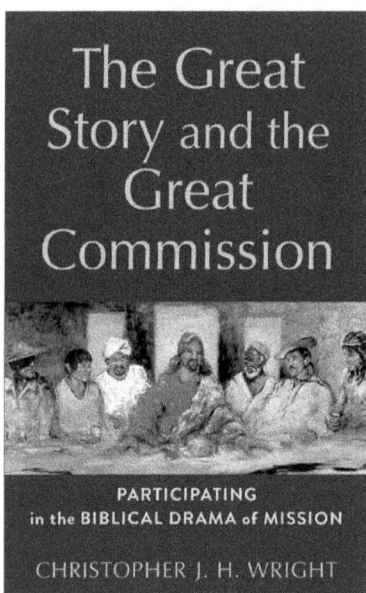

THE GREAT STORY AND THE GREAT COMMISSION

Participating in the Biblical Drama of Mission

by Christopher J. H. Wright
ISBN: 9781540968869
Paperback | 176 pages

Baker Academic

"May we, as God's global people, actively read and respond to this critical teaching"
–Michael Oh, CEO, Lausanne Movement

Learn more at **BakerAcademic.com**

Langham
PARTNERSHIP

Langham Literature and its imprints are a ministry of Langham Partnership.

Langham Partnership is a global fellowship working in pursuit of the vision God entrusted to its founder John Stott –

> *to facilitate the growth of the church in maturity and Christ-likeness through raising the standards of biblical preaching and teaching.*

Our vision is to see churches in the Majority World equipped for mission and growing to maturity in Christ through the ministry of pastors and leaders who believe, teach and live by the word of God.

Our mission is to strengthen the ministry of the word of God through:
• nurturing national movements for biblical preaching
• fostering the creation and distribution of evangelical literature
• enhancing evangelical theological education
especially in countries where churches are under-resourced.

Our ministry

Langham Preaching partners with national leaders to nurture indigenous biblical preaching movements for pastors and lay preachers all around the world. With the support of a team of trainers from many countries, a multi-level programme of seminars provides practical training, and is followed by a programme for training local facilitators. Local preachers' groups and national and regional networks ensure continuity and ongoing development, seeking to build vigorous movements committed to Bible exposition.

Langham Literature provides Majority World preachers, scholars and seminary libraries with evangelical books and electronic resources through publishing and distribution, grants and discounts. The programme also fosters the creation of indigenous evangelical books in many languages, through writer's grants, strengthening local evangelical publishing houses, and investment in major regional literature projects, such as one volume Bible commentaries like *The Africa Bible Commentary* and *The South Asia Bible Commentary*.

Langham Scholars provides financial support for evangelical doctoral students from the Majority World so that, when they return home, they may train pastors and other Christian leaders with sound, biblical and theological teaching. This programme equips those who equip others. Langham Scholars also works in partnership with Majority World seminaries in strengthening evangelical theological education. A growing number of Langham Scholars study in high quality doctoral programmes in the Majority World itself. As well as teaching the next generation of pastors, graduated Langham Scholars exercise significant influence through their writing and leadership.

To learn more about Langham Partnership and the work we do visit **langham.org**

www.ingramcontent.com/pod-product-compliance
Lightning Source LLC
Chambersburg PA
CBHW072045040426
42447CB00012BB/3029